My BRAIN Is Bigger Than Yours

The Truth About Dyslexia

**A RESEARCH-BASED RESOURCE FOR
TEACHERS, PARENTS, & ANY BRAIN INTERESTED IN DYSLEXIA**

SHARON MANDON

Illustrated by Katie Mandon Moore

ISBN 978-1-09839-738-8 (Print)

ISBN 978-1-09839-739-5 (eBook)

Contents

Section One:

A Tale of Two Brains

A True Tale About Dyslexia

We are the Mandon family. Everyone in our home is dyslexic except Tim. That is why we are so interested in dyslexia. We studied up on it and found some remarkably interesting facts we want to share with you!

Our family has decided to view dyslexia not as a learning disability, but as a different way of thinking and learning. That different way of learning comes with strengths and weaknesses. We believe that the disadvantages of being dyslexic are a small rain puddle compared to the huge sea of strengths dyslexic brains possess. Unfortunately, in our society and education model, that puddle can really drown those who cannot get past it. Understanding the challenges and advantages of having a dyslexic brain can change how you feel about dyslexics or about yourself if you are dyslexic.

Our dream for this book is that anyone who reads it would understand dyslexia, more easily identify those who may be dyslexic, and feel empowered to understand and embrace any wonderful dyslexic they are privileged to encounter. Although this book is packed with research-based facts, we purposely made this a short, illustrated, "simple talk" resource to be enjoyed by anyone from dyslexic kiddos to PHD teachers – and anyone in between!

People with dyslexia are sometimes thought of as slow or stupid at school because their reading and spelling are usually awful. Dyslexics are also often thought of as lazy or working below their potential because in areas that do not include reading and spelling, they seem extremely gifted. In this book, I want to share with you the reasons for that.

Dyslexia can be only part of a child's learning challenges. Dyslexia is often linked with things like light sensitivity, eye muscle issues, attention difficulties or other learning struggles. This can be very puzzling to parents and teachers. To help you understand the dyslexia part of the educational puzzle, we want to introduce you to two of our friends.

A Tale of Two Brains!

This is the story of two different brains. One we will call Ally Average Brain*, and the other, Dougie Dyslexic Brain.* Understanding the differences between Dougie and Ally will help you understand dyslexia better.

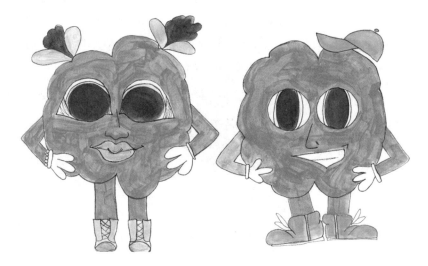

The names and genders of these brains have been changed to protect the innocent. Dyslexia affects boys and girls at approximately the same rate!

Size Matters

Dougie Dyslexic Brain is even bigger than Ally Average Brain.

Ally Average Brain has two lobes.
One is bigger and one is smaller.

Dougie Dyslexic Brain has two lobes also.
His lobes are the same size and both lobes are big.

Dougie Loves Off Roading

Dougie is not only a bigger brain, but he also uses more of his brain when he thinks. Doctors have made special machines that can tell how a brain processes information. Scans by doctors on brains like Ally's actually show that Ally has well-made roads that her thoughts travel on. The scans on dyslexic brains, like Dougie's, show that his thoughts like to go "off road". They don't follow well-worn roads like Ally's thoughts. So, we can actually see and prove that Dougie and Ally process information differently.

Information Processing

Ally processes similar information in the same way and in the same place each time. The information follows well-made roads called nerve paths. When she processes language information, it goes to cool places in her brain that are made to process language. This makes it easier for Ally to learn language.

There is no road to the areas created to process language for Dougie. So, Dougie is forced to use parts of his brain for language that are not designed for language. He often uses the front of his brain, that Ally only uses for decoding new words, to read. Once Ally sees a word that she has seen before, she can zoom the information back to the language processing areas in her brain and remember all about it. Unfortunately, Dougie has to decode words each time he sees them and when he wants to remember information he learned the day before, he has no train to ride to find it. That is because Dougie doesn't process similar information in the same way each time.

He creates nerve paths that are like a bunch of "off road" trails and not superhighways. That makes it harder to find stored information the next time he wants to learn about it.

You can imagine how many wonderful abilities Dougie has because of this. Dougie can problem solve and think out of the box. He can come up with many solutions to the same problem. He is very creative and usually gifted in the arts. He can understand the big picture. He usually has lots of intuition and has great people skills. He can multi-task in many areas. He is often very athletic.

And yet ... school can be his worst nightmare!

This is because when language and spelling enter Dougie's brain, it does not go directly to the language processing areas in his brain. The language information is often processed in the front of Dougie's brain, where Ally processes only words she sees for the first time. This makes reading and spelling, beyond the point where you can just memorize words, almost impossible. Dougie tries to accommodate for this by memorizing shapes of words or looking at the pictures for context clues, but that only works for so long. Soon, there are too many words and no more pictures.

You Hear What I Hear??? Auditory Processing

When Ally hears or sees a word, she hears all the sounds, blends them together and "BAM", she zooms that information back to her language processing areas and immediately reads the word! Yeah!

Unfortunately for Dougie when he is reading, that isn't how it goes. Nothing is wrong with the way Dougie hears, but he processes the sounds differently. The sounds all clump together. This is called an auditory processing problem. So, Dougie tries to sound out a word. The sounds in the word are all clumped together. He does not have the luxury of the word going to the correct areas in his brain. He doesn't hear the individual sounds. His nerve paths take the information to a part of his brain that was not made for reading. You can see why he has trouble figuring out words!

Do You See What I See?? No! Directionality

Whenever I say I am dyslexic, people always think that means I see or write backwards. Let me explain why that is.

Ally gets information and is not confused by which way things go. She has an internal idea of what right vs. left is, up vs. down is and things like that.

Dougie does not have that internal compass. Dougie is very confused about which way things go. This is called a problem with directionality. He may see "DOG" and process it "GOD". He may write things backwards. He may be very confused over his left and right. He may never be able to keep track of the hands of a clock or remember in which order to say or write his numbers. These issues are very normal for children until about second grade. However, if they continue indefinitely, you can imagine all the ways this could make school difficult for Dougie.

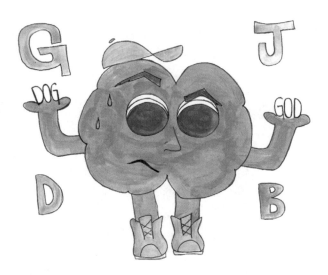

Although dyslexics have these challenges because of the way their brains are wired, they also have many advantages. We like to think of it this way. Being dyslexic gives you a puddle of problems and a sea of strengths. A dyslexic may come up with seventeen different moves in basketball for the same shot. He may paint a rose in a different way than anyone has before him. He may think of a cure for cancer that no one had even considered. He may come up with a new form of poetry. He may figure out how to fix his roof without any of the usual supplies. He may invent the "next big thing"! *Think of what the world might miss if Dougie decides he is dumb in grade school.*

It's a Family Affair

Dyslexia runs in families. It is called hereditary. If you are dyslexic, then some close relative is too. (Although, they may not even know it!) This is great because you can understand each other. Many times, a family of dyslexics is said to speak their own language. (… usually replacing nouns and other details they have trouble finding in their brains with "that thingy over there") Unfortunately, coming from a family of dyslexics can also be hard because most dyslexic's don't have an easy time with school work, so often dyslexic parents cannot help dyslexic students with their homework.

Just Say NO to More of the Same!

About 80% of the population is not dyslexic and learns how to read and spell in a similar way. So, it makes sense that everyone is taught that way. But now that you understand dyslexia better, you can see why that just won't work for Dougie. You can do more drills, get conventional tutoring, humiliate him, try to motivate him or whatever you want, but Dougie cannot learn the same way Ally can. *More of the same is not helpful.* It actually discourages Dougie from wanting to try or exhausts him, so he loses his focus. Therefore, dyslexic people often develop low self-esteem. They think they are stupid. Some people assume they are lazy or aren't trying because basic schoolwork seems so easy to a non-dyslexic, and dyslexics are often very bright and articulate in most parts of their lives and excel socially. These mixed signals can be confusing to the dyslexic person and the ones trying to help them.

Approximately 1 out of every 5 people are dyslexic!

Help Wanted!!!!!!!!!!

However, people can be very wrong about Dougie! He is usually smart and a hard worker if you give him tools to use. These tools can be taught by *a specific tutor or teacher who understands dyslexia.* These specialists use very specific methods to help. You usually do not find this kind of tutoring at a tutoring center. Some schools provide this kind of help, and some do not. If yours does not, please provide it for your child. It costs less than braces for the child's teeth in most cases and can change their academic life forever!

First, dyslexia specialists address the auditory processing condition. Dougie learns how to break down sounds. This is hard work but can be done.

Second, it has been discovered through special brain scans that Dougie can create a nerve path to his language processing areas. (The older a brain gets, the harder it is to make these new paths.) Dyslexia specialists can help Dougie do this by working on specific kinds of activities and drills with him.

Third, dyslexia tutors can teach Dougie very specific spelling rules to compensate for his inability to remember which letters go in which order when spelling a word.

Variety Is the Spice of Life

Dyslexics add so much to our world and our classrooms! There are so many little things besides tutoring that help dyslexics, but they require a change in thinking. One size does not fit all. Recognizing, understanding and developing strategies to help Dougie meet his full potential is very important … just ask these brains

Section Two:
Lost in Dyslexia-Ville

Learning the Warning Signs
That You May Be Dyslexic

Now that you have taken some time to understand what dyslexia really is in section one, the next step is to figure out who in your world might be dyslexic. *Luckily, because of years of research, we know a lot of the signs of dyslexia. Unfortunately, those signs are not familiar to many important people - like teachers, parents, and many dyslexics themselves!* Keep in mind, no two people are the same, so not all dyslexics will have the same symptoms or severity of difficulty in school. Also, not all students with learning difficulties are dyslexic. Helping you read the signs that point to "Dyslexia – ville" and who might live there is the purpose of this section.

I am Sharon Mandon. I remember hearing the word dyslexic used about me vaguely as a child. I thought that was why I wrote my "S" backwards until second grade. Other than that, I had no idea what it meant. I went through grade school in the 70's. My school was really into "Free to Be You and Me!", and that worked great for me. I have specific memories of being told I was lazy and that I did not live up to my potential. I remember I was embarrassed by teachers who put up spelling charts with stars because I was the only student with no stars. I remember peers who called me an air head because I did normal dyslexic things. I spent grade school with my desk next to the teachers. Unlike most dyslexic girls, I definitely did not fade into the background. I was more like a typical boy in my reaction. (Typically, female dyslexics tend to withdraw, and male dyslexics tend to act out. Of course, this varies by person.) I acted out, talked, wrote notes, planned pranks, and basically distracted the class! I was voted class clown in grade school and most fun to be around in my High School yearbook. However, I was a great listener when I wanted to be and could listen and take great notes. That is how I passed tests as I got older. I also did all my assignments, so when I could not pass some tests, I still passed classes. In college I would often not even buy the textbooks because they were expensive, and I really didn't get much from reading them. Instead, I would create study groups and quiz everyone else using my notes. I learned best by discussing the content. That is the way I got through my college classes. I graduated from college and became a teacher. As a teacher, I sometimes felt like an imposter. I was applauded for my classroom control and my ability to reach diverse students. My class was fun, engaging and a great place to learn. However, I had to read through things right before I taught a lesson, or I sometimes forgot the details. I would pay my students with our classroom currency if they would politely point out anything I misspelled. One time I got chastised in front of my staff by an older teacher for misspelling a word on the notes I was asked to take for the meeting. (I was 23 and she was probably in her 50's) She said she was appalled at the skills of young teachers coming out of college. These are just some of the things a dyslexic faces in a world that is ignorant about dyslexia. I got through my higher education because I had learned so many tricks to compensate for my dyslexia by that age. I was not highly supported in my chaotic home regarding my education, but I felt like if I tried and got a B or a C, it was fine. God blessed me with a strong will, a good sense of humor, and good social skills. I wish I would have understood my dyslexia. *I'm not sure I would have made it through K-12 school with any confidence left to move on if I had attended when my kids were in school. (starting in the mid 90's) With the constant assessments based on spitting out random facts, pushing concepts in reading and math into the lower grades, and the pressure in our society to get straight A's, dyslexics have really suffered. Luckily for dyslexics, and all students in my opinion, there has been a shift in education back toward valuing multi-sensory learning, discussion, reasoning and thinking skills. This is a much better learning environment for a dyslexic.*

I didn't know anything about my own dyslexia or how to help my dyslexic students as I began to teach. I look back and see faces of students I could have helped so much more if I had only known how to identify dyslexic students and had the tools to teach them well.

I had three daughters and never gave dyslexia much thought. My girls passed all the preschool milestones ahead of schedule. They were talkative, funny, very inquisitive and physically agile. In my motherly love, I knew they would buzz through school and become whatever they wanted to be …

… and they would have, if it didn't require learning to read and spell!!!!!!!!!!

I got the dreaded "Call" at different times for each of my kids. The "Your child is having problems" … call. "Sarah is one of the best students in my 4th grade class, but because of her reading score, we need to have you sign this possibility of retention form." "Katie is reading at a level four and should be at a level twelve. We want to retain her." "Bethany works so hard. Can I give her an effort report card and give you her real report card, so she won't be sad?" These are actual quotes from very caring, hardworking teachers.

I felt so terrible that I was a teacher myself and could not help my own kids. I decided to do whatever it took to figure out a way. My journey to figuring out what was going on lead me to listening to Dyslexia lectures by Susan Barton of Bright Solutions for Dyslexia. (We will always be grateful to her for her pivotal contributions to helping the dyslexic community) About five hours in, I could barely hold back the tears. For the first time in my life, I felt that I understood myself and what my kids were going through. The signs had all been there. I just didn't know the signs. Susan Barton gave us a list of warning signs. I went through and marked each one that my children or I had. We each had an amazing amount of the signs showing that we were dyslexic.

In this section I will be telling you about the warning signs we missed for so long. As you read about us, maybe you will see yourself or someone you love. "Dyslexia-ville" is not a wasteland. It just has a different landscape. A beautiful, wonderful, yet sometimes rugged landscape! Don't be alarmed if you see signs that are leading there!

Keep this in mind, if a student struggles with reading and spelling, there may be lots of reasons for it. However, if the student is otherwise bright and they also have three or more of these warning signs - It would be a good idea to have the student tested for dyslexia.

Lost in Dyslexia – Ville

Hi! I am Dougie Dyslexic Brain, and this is my friend Ally Average Brain. Remember us? Both of us have things we are great at and things that are harder for us because of the way we process information. About four out of five brains work like Ally. About one out of five brains work like me, Dougie. A lot of times school can be harder for brains like mine. That is why it is important to know if you think like Ally or me. Once you know that, there are ways to make school a better place for you to reach your highest potential. That is why Ally and I are going to tell you signs you can easily spot that could mean you think like me, Dougie Dyslexic Brain.

First, let me tell you a little story about Ally and me. Ally Average Brain and I were the best of friends. Our parents were friends when we were born, and we grew up together.

We were both extremely bright and wonderful. On the first day of school, we held hands as we walked into kindergarten. We were in the same class; we had the same lunch box and we sat in desks that were next to each other.

As school progressed, it was obvious that while Ally was excelling, I, Dougie, was falling behind. No one understood how this could be. Ally, as well as parents and teachers, tried to help me. Nothing that worked for Ally seemed to help me learn. It was like we lived in worlds that looked the same, but the names of the streets were all different. Ally tried to get me to walk down Phonics Blvd, and I was stuck on Clumped Sound Street. Ally tried to get me to put the words I read on a speed train toward my language processing areas, but all I could find was a quad on a four-wheel driving path. It was all so confusing to everyone. Weren't we the same? We seemed like it … until reading and spelling came into the picture!

All along the road, Dougie saw warning signs like "Hazardous Spelling Zone", "Hard to Tie Shoes Area", and "Right and Left Confusion Warning". Those warning signs could have helped Dougie and all the people around him realize that he did not live and learn in Average-ville with Ally. Dougie actually lived in Dyslexia-ville and that is why the directions he was receiving were leaving him feeling more and more lost. He could get to where he needed to be … Reading Road, Spelling Expressway and Success in School Street, but it was going to take different directions for him to do it!

That is why knowing the warning signs is so important, because then someone like Dougie can figure out how to get to where he needs to go. He can find his learning sweet spot!

Ally and Dougie have three friends that are great kids like them, and who happen to think like Dougie. These cool brains want to introduce you to their friends and tell you about the mystery they faced when they went to school. All of them were having trouble in school. It was because they lived in Dylsexia-ville with Dougie and didn't know it either. Our hope is that as you learn about them recognizing the warning signs they had and getting different directions, you may see yourself or someone you know. The first step is realizing you are dyslexic. If you are, then you can figure out how to live your best life and learn in Dylexia – ville.

Katie - The Wonderful Creative Type!

Hi! I'm Katie. I'm dyslexic, but we didn't figure that out or how to help me until I was in fourth grade. By that time, I felt horribly stressed about school and myself. There were clues we could have noticed. I had a ton of the strengths of a dyslexic. I am very artistic. I am very creative and articulate. I am musical. I have a wonderful sense of humor. I also had lots of the signs that I might be dyslexic and might have a hard time in school. I am thankful we figured out I was dyslexic and got the help I needed. I am going to tell you some of the clues that helped me realize I belonged in Dyslexia-ville with Dougie.

Before I Started School

WARNING SIGN ONE
I Mixed Up the Sounds in My Words

I started speaking well at a very young age. A lot of times dyslexic kids don't speak early. However, I mixed up the sounds in many of my words. My favorite mix up was that I called "nail polish", "paul nailish". My sisters did the same thing. My older sister Sarah called the telephone, "ca-cone". Our family called it that for years.

WARNING SIGN TWO
It Took Me a Long Time to Pick a Dominant Hand

I couldn't decide if I wanted to be left-handed or right-handed. I would write with my right hand and kick with my left foot. I would eat with either hand.

Once I Started School

WARNING SIGN THREE
I Reversed My Letters and Numbers

Left and right were always confusing for me. I wrote my b's and d's backwards until yesterday! (Only worry if a child does this past 1st grade!) I could accidentally write an entire sentence as a mirror image and write the next sentence in the correct way.

In math I would know every step to solve a problem and understand the concept completely. Unfortunately, I would come up with answers that were way off. My mom became a professional at finding the place I mixed up the steps or wrote the digits in the wrong order.

!eitaK ma I

Who are you?

WARNING SIGN FOUR
Reading Was Extremely Draining to Me

Reading made me feel exhausted. It took so much concentration and energy. After a while I would start yawning and then I would start staring into space. Some people thought I was daydreaming or not trying to pay attention. The truth is that I just had to have a break. *No one would think anything if someone with one leg took a rest while climbing Mt. Everest. Reading felt like climbing Mt. Everest with one leg to me.*

WARNING SIGN FIVE
I Began to Hate School!

I went from loving school and being a social bee, to hating school, and having very few friends by third grade. This was definitely a horrible time for me. I would have nightmares about school and felt sick to my stomach when I was there. I felt so bad about myself because I thought I was dumb. (Studies show that the shame a child experiences regarding being dyslexic and feeling unable to perform in school is as high as a child that is being seriously abused.)

WARNING SIGN SIX
I Can't Read Complicated Music

Our whole family is musical. We love to sing, listen to music, and dance. Unfortunately, reading music is really hard for us. Sarah and I both took up an instrument. We loved it until the music got complicated. My mom had the same experience in school. We can play by ear and memorize songs, but we can't read complicated music while playing it.

These are just some of the clues we had that I was dyslexic. Now that I know what dyslexia is and all the great things about it, it makes it easier to work through the hard parts. I went through book one and two of the Barton Reading and Spelling Program. My mom was my tutor for that, but it became too hard for her to do book 3 and 4 because she is dyslexic too! So, I went through a year of Linda Mood Bell tutoring with Jinny.

Our wonderful tutor!

Just like every human, I am unique. Part of my learning journey was figuring out I needed eye therapy as well as dyslexia tutoring. My eyes would get tired and sometimes when I took my eye screening exam, they would think I was "messing around". I finally got to a developmental ophthalmologist and discovered my eye muscles were underdeveloped. This made tracking almost impossible, and when I read, the lines would move! Focusing was very exhausting. This was a huge piece of my learning puzzle. It is important to remember that dyslexia might only be part of a person's learning challenges. Getting this issue corrected was pivotal in my academic success.

I am now all grown up! Grade school was difficult. I was homeschooled from 4th to 7th grade. These were the years I got very specific help with my dyslexia and did eye therapy. (If you have a child who is struggling with reading, it is a particularly good idea to have them checked for eye muscle issues by a developmental ophthalmologist.) I got a 504 plan at my public distance learning Charter School to help me with state testing. (Standardized tests can be very stressful for a dyslexic student and in many cases are not an accurate representation of what they know.) As a transition back to school, I went to a Montessori Charter school for 8th grade. I went to my very academic local High School and graduated with a 3.2 GPA. I excelled in choir, dance, and art. I went to Community College for my GE and then went away to Grand Canyon University – where I graduated Magna Cum Laude with a degree in Communication. I completed college in four years. (When my sisters and I began college, it was the first time we ever got real accommodations for dyslexia in class. You can reach out to the Student Services department to get qualified for help if you are a dyslexic college student. They will need to see your diagnosis paperwork or a copy of your High School IEP or 504. If you do not have those forms, they will test you at most Jr Colleges for free.) I currently teach ESL and run a cool ETSY page featuring the jewelry and crafts I make. (Many artists are dyslexic.) My advice to a dyslexic student is to embrace who you are. You may do things differently, but different can be absolutely amazing. Dyslexia makes school hard, but it makes lots of things in life great if you embrace your creativity and outside of the box thinking skills. Own your quirky greatness.

Sarah - The Strong Athlete

Hi, I am Sarah. I'm dyslexic. School was always hard for me, but teachers didn't really notice my struggles till I was in fourth grade. The reading got harder and the textbooks got more confusing. I had used my dyslexic strengths to get me through until that point. I am a very good listener and a hard worker. I am also good at working in groups. I always had a great time at recess playing sports. I planned fun activities and pranks for my friends. I had warning signs of dyslexia, but like Katie, we didn't know the signs. Here are some of the signs we missed.

WARNING SIGN ONE
Chronic Ear Infections

As a baby I had one ear infection after another. I finally got put on antibiotics daily for a long time. Who knew that could be a sign of dyslexia!

WARNING SIGN TWO
I Hated Rhymes!

Most little kids love rhyming books or try to rhyme things. I have always hated it. That may be because it was impossible for me to do! When I was asked to tell which word rhymed, I could not. I just didn't hear it, and that made me get mad!

Once I Started School

WARNING SIGN THREE
I Hated to Read Out Loud!

The reason for this is that I read very inaccurately and slow. I left out words all the time, especially small ones like of, I, or if. I was the queen of substituting a word I knew for one I didn't know, even if it made no sense at all! For example, if it said, "She was late quite a bit." I might read it, "She was late quiet bit." This made me feel embarrassed and not want to read out loud!

WARNING SIGN FOUR
I Hate There, Their and They're!

I had such a hard time with homonyms. I could never remember which spelling went with which meaning. It still bugs me! Any spelling test was hard for me, but the ones that had homonyms on them were the worst.

WARNING SIGN FIVE
I Can't Tell Left from Right

Saying "Which right?" seems normal in our household. Only my dad is really sure of his left and right. Having a problem with this and other directional things is common for dyslexics and can be hard. We went on a family trip around the country and only my dad was good with the map. I had a very painful experience where I was chosen by my peers to be the Mate on the CA Thayer. The Thayer was a restored sailing boat in the San Francisco Bay. Mates lead the crew and answered to the Captain. Learning the sides of the ship was so hard for me and the captain yelled at me in front of my whole class for not taking my job seriously because I didn't know which side was port and which was starboard. I had studied and tried, but it was very confusing to me. It was one of my most awful school moments.

When we figured out I was dyslexic, we realized that I couldn't hear separate sounds at all. My mom took me out of school, and I was home-schooled, so we could focus on my specific needs. (She did this for all of us for as long as we needed it.) I went to a tutor who used a program from Linda Mood Bell to teach me to hear individual sounds. I had to learn how my tongue moved with different sound combinations in order to really learn the sounds. I was the only one in my family who needed this kind of tutoring. After that tutoring, I did books one and two of the Barton Reading and Spelling System. I could not believe the difference. I often refer to my life as "before tutoring" and "after tutoring". That is because it was a hard and confusing time before I got help. Once I knew I was dyslexic and understood how to excel in "Dyslexia-ville", it was like a different world at school.

I'm all grown up now! In High School I played basketball and volley-ball and I graduated from a very academic school with a 3.89 GPA. I got a school wide award for being such a hard-working student. Sophomore year was a bit harder because I took a foreign language. (Which is often tough for dyslexic students) That was my only C in High School. (In college I took ASL as a second language and loved it. This is a great option for dyslexics since they often excel in sign language.) I enjoyed sports, photography, and advanced choir during my High School career, as well as earning honor-able mention for my community service. (All of which are usual strengths for a dyslexic!) I went to community college and got an AA in Biological

Science. I then went away to Grand Canyon University and got my BS in nursing. (Dyslexics make wonderful health care professionals because they often have intuitive, engaging people skills and they can figure out complicated situations because of their problem-solving strengths. However, the schooling is often particularly difficult for them) I am an RN. Dealing with Dyslexia is still a part of my life, but when I learned about my brain and how it worked, I gained confidence in my strengths and my ability to compensate for my weaknesses. That has made school and life so much better for me. I would tell a dyslexic student to find and be proud to use any study method that works for you. In college I walked for hours memorizing body systems, used a huge white board to draw and redraw things I had to know, and made my own videos during labs to help me remember information for the tests. My mom advocated for me as a dyslexic student in K-12 by supporting me at home. I had to advocate for myself in college to get teachers to follow the accommodations. I have been shamed by teachers who were ignorant about dyslexia. My advice to a dyslexic student is to understand and embrace dyslexia and stand up for yourself at school and in life. I also want to encourage you to *figure out your tools and use them!*

Bethany - The All-Around Social Wonder!

Hi! I am Bethany. Because I am the youngest in my family, we recognized the warning signs for my dyslexia very early. My sisters had paved the way to "dyslexia-ville" for me. That has been a huge help for me in school. By first grade I was already getting specialized help. (Early detection and help for students make things easier for everyone … particularly the student! I also had lots of the wonderful parts of being dyslexic.) I have always had a way with people and am a born leader. I was so articulate and personable as a young child that if I answered the phone at age three, people would leave long messages with me because they thought I was ten. My second-grade teacher was sure I would be the first female president of the US. (And I would be in good company because lots of former presidents were also dyslexic!) Because I was able to listen well, and I was so young, my dyslexia never really made me feel too bad or behind at school. I got the help I needed early. These were some of the warning signs I had that I belonged in dyslexia – ville with my sisters.

Before I Started School

WARNING SIGN ONE
My Close Relatives Are Dyslexic

As I just said, my mom and sisters are dyslexic. I also have dyslexic grandparents, uncles, and cousins! Many people don't realize that dyslexia is the reason they did poorly in school or think certain ways, but once you understand dyslexia and the warning signs, you can often see it in your family tree.

WARNING SIGN TWO
Big Reactions to Childhood Illnesses

I did not get sick a lot as a child, but when I did … I really did! Things would turn into infections or flare up my asthma. My sister Katie did this too. Strep throat turned into Scarlet Fever for her.

Bethany with a bad case of the chicken pox!

WARNING SIGN THREE
I Had a Hard Time Learning to Tie Shoes

I could not tie my shoes the regular way! My mom wouldn't let us get Velcro shoes until we learned to tie regular shoes with strings, so I worked hard on this skill. Finally, we found a bunny story with less steps that taught me to tie a bow. Then I could tie my shoes with no problem! (Songs, stories, and riddles often help dyslexic's do tasks that they might not be able to do easily!)

Once I Started School

WARNING SIGN FOUR
My Spelling Was Terrible!

Spelling became an issue for me in Kindergarten. I am extremely competitive. In my class, only when we could spell our names correctly, could we take our name card off our desk. I was the last kid to have my name tag still on my desk and I never got to take it off the whole year! *I hated that*! In general, my sister's and I are horrible spellers!

WARNING SIGN FIVE
I Can't Tell Time on a Clock with Hands!

I really struggled in class with "time math"! I secretly wanted to rip the plastic hands off the clocks they gave us to practice with! It was so confusing for me. I also got a watch for my birthday with hands and begged to return it for a digital! (And I did)

WARNING SIGN SIX
Random Facts Are Hard to Memorize

Memorizing random facts was not going to happen with me. Memorizing the multiplication tables, days of the week, and the names of letters was so hard. Fortunately, setting random facts to music helped me with all the big categories. Still, random stuff for Science or History, like dates or tables, really makes me struggle.

WARNING SIGN SEVEN
I Can't Think of the Names of Things

In our house, I am not alone. We rarely say a sentence that doesn't include the words "that thing" in the place of the name of the item we are talking about. My Grandma (who is not dyslexic) says we all speak a different language at our house. That is because she lives in "Average-Ville" and doesn't speak "Dyslexic-ese!"

I am all grown up now! As we said, early detection and help with my dyslexia was an advantage of all of us living in "dyslexia-ville" together. It made school so much easier for me. I went through Books One and Two of the Barton Reading and Spelling System in first grade. Then I went to a year and a half of Linda Mood Bell tutoring using the Seeing Stars workbooks. (So did my sister Katie) As with my sisters, we have also done lots of other things that helped me excel. In grade school I got numerous "Character Awards" for hard work and respect for others. I graduated High School with a 3.8 GPA and received a scholarship to play volleyball in college. (Many dyslexics are great at sports!) Volleyball took lots of my time in High School, but I also enjoyed advanced choir. I graduated from college with honors. I now have a BA in Liberal Studies and a CA teaching credential. I teach 1st grade at a local public school. (Dyslexics are often great teachers because they can do and think about so much all at once and they are fantastic at figuring out how to reach a diverse group in a classroom) My advice to a dyslexic student is to remember that your best is enough. You will not be good at specific things in school because of your dyslexia, but you are a precious, gifted person anyway. Let your mistakes help you do better the next time and give you empathy and understanding regarding the weaknesses of others. Rock your mad skills and use your big dyslexic mind to overcome your weak spots.

Have you seen yourself or someone you love in our story?

**Has a mystery been solved about why you are lost
at school or someone who you love is?**

Do you realize now that you may be living in "dyslexia-ville"?

Knowledge is power!

*Understanding is the first step toward getting help!
(Moms tend to be a dyslexic's number one ally)*

**Above all, enjoy who you are and the
wonderful land of "Dyslexia-ville"!**

Warning Signs
of Dyslexia

Attached is a list of warning signs from Bright Solutions for Dyslexia. *If a child has 3 or more of the following warning signs, encourage that child's parents and teachers to learn more about dyslexia.*

In Preschool

- delayed speech

- mixing up the sounds and syllables in long words

- chronic ear infections

- severe reactions to childhood illnesses

- constant confusion of left versus right

- late establishing a dominant hand

- difficulty learning to tie shoes

- trouble memorizing their address, phone number, or the alphabet

- can't create words that rhyme

- a close relative with dyslexia

In Elementary School

- dysgraphia (slow, non-automatic handwriting that is difficult to read)

- letter or number reversals continuing past the end of first grade

- extreme difficulty learning cursive

- slow, choppy, inaccurate reading:
  - guesses based on shape or context
  - skips or misreads prepositions (at, to, of)
  - ignores suffixes
  - can't sound out unknown words

- terrible spelling

- often can't remember sight words (they, were, does) or homonyms (their, they're, and there)

- difficulty telling time with a clock with hands

- trouble with math
  - memorizing multiplication tables
  - memorizing a sequence of steps
  - directionality

- when speaking, difficulty finding the correct word
  - lots of "whatyamacallits" and "thingies"
  - common sayings come out slightly twisted

- extremely messy bedroom, backpack, and desk

- dreads going to school
  - complains of stomach aches or headaches
  - may have nightmares about school

In High School
All of the above symptoms plus:

- limited vocabulary

- extremely poor written expression
  - large discrepancy between verbal skills and written compositions

- unable to master a foreign language

- difficulty reading printed music

- poor grades in many classes

- may drop out of high school

In Adults
Education history similar to above, plus:

- slow reader

- may have to read a page 2 or 3 times to understand it

- terrible speller

- difficulty putting thoughts onto paper
  - dreads writing memos or letters

- still has difficulty with right versus left

- often gets lost, even in a familiar city

- sometimes confuses b and d, especially when tired or sick

Bright Solutions for Dyslexia
Email: info@BrightSolutions.US
(408) 559-3652
Copyright © 2002 by Susan Barton. All Rights Reserved.
Reprinted with permission by Susan Barton

Section Three:
Give Me Strategies
or Give Me F's!

DOUGLAS HENRY
Tips to Help Your Favorite Dyslexic!

Introduction

Have it your way at Learning King. Don't we wish! Burger King has a much easier job then educators today. Unfortunately, our schools and teachers are faced with the most diverse set of challenges ever. Many of these problems are societal and solutions are hard to find. The good news is that with all the research done on dyslexia, so many tools and strategies are available to help dyslexic students. Since about one out of five students is dyslexic and solutions are available to meet their educational challenges, I say we go for it! We need to understand dyslexia first. Then we need to embrace a change in thinking to include these bright wonderful students. Here are some strategies we found extremely helpful! However, don't feel limited to these ideas. Once you understand dyslexia and begin to see how simple changes can really help, we hope you will think of creative ideas of your own to help your favorite dyslexic. Together we can tap into this huge asset hiding in our homes and classrooms.

Specialized tutoring is especially important for Dougie to become proficient in reading and spelling but getting that may not be possible. (Sadly, if the district a child lives in does not provide screenings and a comprehensive multisensory phonics intervention program for dyslexics, the burden to assess and get help for them falls on the parents. If the parents are under resourced or uninvolved, the student is left to flounder. What a terrible loss of potential and what an unnecessary burden for the dyslexic student to bear!) However, even without tutoring, there are ways to enhance Dougie's learning experience. Here are some of the strategies we have found to be helpful.

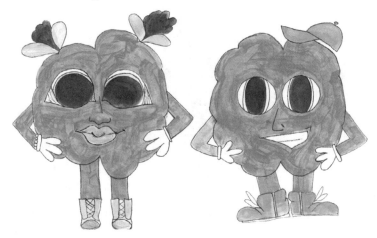

Dougie Dyslexic Brain and Ally Average Brain
want to share strategies that may help dyslexics.

Just Say No to ... Memorizing Random Facts!

Dougie has a SUPER hard time memorizing random information. We need to find ways to help him with this. One way to help him is ... **Music!**

Any information that is put to a tune seems easier for Dougie to remember. Tunes can be used for math facts, vocabulary, memorizing literature, memorizing addresses and phone numbers, and even the steps in long division. The list goes on and on!

Math concepts are often a strength of Dougie's. Unfortunately, due to how he processes information, that is not always obvious. To get from knowing the correct concept to computing the correct answer, Dougie needs to memorize facts and steps in a specific order. He has to write digits in the right order and sometimes copy them again. This is a mine field for Dougie! However, finding the following programs did help us.

One great resource for learning multiplication tables is the skip counting tapes by Math U See. These tapes put the multiplication facts set to music. Math U See also teaches number sense in a wonderfully multi-sensory way. Touch Math is another program that may help. With little children, they use fingers and touch points. Touch Math now has ways to teach long multiplication and division in a short form that is much easier for Dougie. My kids did fine in math until they got to long multiplication and division. Unfortunately, many dyslexics get stuck there too and lose confidence in their math ability. Once we taught our children the short methods, they were much more accurate. Small changes like these can make remarkable differences in Dougie's mathematical success.

We Hate Webster!

Spelling is such an issue for Dougie. Looking up words in the dictionary is ridiculously difficult for many dyslexics. Ally sometimes doesn't understand.

But there are no easy answers for Dougie's spelling!

To look up words in a dictionary, he must figure out alphabetical order and know at least the basic order of the letters in the word he wants to spell. Problems with directionality and problems with random memorization really foil looking things up for Dougie.

Spell check can also be a problem. Dougie doesn't know which of the words that show up on the screen as an option is the one that he wants to spell. He often spells things so badly that the computer can't even recognize the word. So, the spell check idea is hard too.

Studying spelling lists is sometimes helpful for tests. Dougie can put a lot of energy in and memorize words right before a test. Unfortunately, recalling those words for future use in writing does not often happen. Learning spelling rules is a better way, but even those are easily forgotten. This is very frustrating for Dougie and for Ally, who can't understand why Dougie doesn't know how to spell. When Dougie is so caught up in trying to spell, he can't concentrate on important stuff like what he was trying to express in writing. This is such a shame because Dougie is usually highly creative and could have great content in his writing!

Don't Despair!

There is help for Dougie's spelling. First, there are *handheld talking dictionaries*. You type in or say a word. The machine does all kinds of stuff. It gives you correct spellings like spell check, but the difference is that it reads the choices of words to you. This gives Dougie a way to know he is looking at the word he wanted to spell. These devices also give definitions and even show Dougie how a word looks in cursive. What a bonanza for a Dougie! (Although, copying the word off the screen correctly onto the paper isn't always going to happen! ☺) Computers have many apps that can do these same functions.

Second, there are many computer programs that offer voice to text features. It works by the computer typing whatever you say. Now Dougie, who often has wonderfully creative ideas, can get them on paper without it being so hard. These tools can help Dougie feel more confident and focus on his other wonderful language arts strengths.

Pencils and Pens Are Not Our Friends!

Sometimes a dyslexic will have a hard time even holding a pen or pencil. He often holds the pencil wrong and squeezes it really hard to control it. This can cause his hand to cramp. He may never remember the correct place to start printing a letter or how to correctly shape it. Cursive is usually even worse. He often isn't sure of margins and letter spacing, no matter how hard he tries. You may not be able to read his writing at all. Practice doesn't always "make perfect" with Dougie. This problem is called dysgraphia and many dyslexics have it in some form.

Dougie needs to learn to write. This will not be fun for him. But he also needs to be able to have a way to freely express his thoughts in a written form. That is where typing can help. Teaching Dougie to type on a tablet or laptop with larger keys can really be helpful. It gives Dougie time where he is not feeling tortured by his pencil, and he is free to think of content information. The computer programs we discussed (voice to text programs) that type what Dougie says can do wonders in this area as well.

Books on Tape Rock

Have you ever been forced to read something that was really boring? Have you had to read it over and over? That is what happens to Dougie. His reading ability level is way below his interest level. No wonder he hates to read. It is really hard, and the stories hold no interest for him. His reading level keeps him from learning age-appropriate ideas and concepts while reading. It limits his vocabulary severely. It takes away his joy in literature ... but, it doesn't have to!

Ally may be well intentioned ... but she is wrong about Dougie. Dougie's struggles in reading have nothing to do with not being exposed to books. He may, with time and specialized help, become a wonderful reader. However, he may never read well. He is not lazy, but he is not dumb either. He will, sooner or later, decide that what he can read is below his intelligence and stop doing it. However, listening to books on tape can help any dyslexic on their journey toward academic achievement and becoming a well-rounded, educated person.

This is also very important for textbooks that are required reading. Having required books on tape gives Dougie a chance to learn the content and hopefully pass the class! Hearing or reading books is wonderful for any student. It not only improves their vocabulary, but it gets them familiar with the sound of wonderful writing, which is one of the keys to becoming a wonderful writer. Hearing books read out loud opens Dougie's mind to concepts and ideas that he may never have explored if he had to be able to read the material himself.

Yes, Dougie must learn to read, but he must also have a reason to. I think I tried so hard to read well because my mom loved to read and read to me. I wanted to do it too. Books on tape can hook Dougie on reading.

I had my children read along with some of their books on tape. I also had all their textbooks on tape when they were struggling to understand the text. We also just listened to about a million fun stories for no reason except to enjoy them. It made an amazing difference in my children's performance in school.

What Really Matters?

One day my high school history teacher, who was a great storyteller, kept me after class. He told me how amazed he was by my essay answers. He said it was like reading his lecture off my test. He probably wondered at all the dates and names I had gotten wrong on the main part of my test, while being able to recite his stories word for word. I wondered myself. Now I understand why!

Dougie has an amazing ability to see the whole picture. He understands the deeper meaning of a story. He sees cause and effect. He remembers things in the context of a story. These are amazing qualities for understanding science concepts or lessons we need to learn from history. However, most tests in those subjects focus on the random facts. Dates, names, tables, isolated vocabulary, timelines ... does that sound familiar??? A year after taking a test, almost no one remembers that kind of information. What really counts is if Ally and Dougie remember the concepts and applications found in history and science. They can always look up the random facts later if they need them.

Don't Hold Me Back

Once Dougie can listen to his textbooks on tape, what if you gave him tests that had key words, dates, timelines, etc. provided for him. What if you then asked hard questions about some scientific principal or how the events of a time period affected a people group or the world today? I believe you would be shocked at the depth of his answers! (*No points off for misspelling please!*) That is one more accommodation that can be easily executed and can really boost Dougie's performance and self-confidence about school. Another option is allowing a dyslexic student to have a 3x5 card, with all the random facts they can fit on it, available to them during tests. Not only is making this card a very useful way to study, but it will also greatly increase Dougie's performance.

Simply Label!

Dyslexic's often have a hard time getting organized. You can see why since they think in such a random way. Often parents and teachers think Dougie is bucking the system, when really, he can't remember lots of random rules or where you want stuff put back. How can we help? First, it helps to keep rules simple and to the point. Then it helps to post the rules and his schedule somewhere obvious to Dougie. Next, it is very helpful to keep Dougie's stuff to a minimum. Have a place for everything and label the spot. These strategies have helped us amazingly at our home. You can also write out lists of what you want done so Dougie can remember. (This can be a list of what he needs to do to get ready for bed, what tasks are included when cleaning the bathroom or even each part of a school assignment you want him to complete.)

Tick, Tock! Stop That Clock!

A huge problem for most dyslexics is that they just run out of time! Homework takes them forever! Tests take them longer than the allotted time! You must remember that dyslexics are doing a lot of work to read and process language. Then they are trying to find with the content they learned on their four-wheeler. No wonder it takes them longer. Simply giving a dyslexic student more time on assignments and tests can do wonders for their scores. Also, if you break up a long assignment into little parts that take less time and where the student can have a break in between tasks, it is greatly beneficial.

Right Way – My Way

One thing I have found is that dyslexics often do things differently than non-dyslexics. Non-dyslexics tend to do things the same way each time and consider their way to be the "right way". They may not realize they feel that way or be willing to admit it, but they often do. This is not a good mind set for the boss, friend, teacher, or parent of a dyslexic. The strength of the dyslexic is that they make accommodations for their weaknesses and come up with great new ways to do things. If they are in a rigid environment, they cannot use this strength and may feel extremely frustrated! Instead, I challenge everyone to think …

If It Works, It Is the Right Way!
If a dyslexic is given this freedom,
they tend to do better in all areas of their lives.

Multisensory Learning – YES!

Dyslexics learn best in a multisensory way! Pen and paper can get boring. Some fun ways to work on phonics review or spelling are:

- to use a tray that has salt, sand, flour, or something like that and have the student write in it

- to use a laser pointer on the wall or floor

- to put shaving cream in a zip lock bag and write the word

- to write in the dirt with a stick

- to use a white board

- to use a window pen on a window or glass slider

Hear My Cry
Or I'll Give You Something to Cry About!

Being a teacher or parent is an incredibly hard job! Really learning to understand dyslexia and implementing solutions may seem overwhelming. Unfortunately, Dougie will not usually be ignored. He often cannot do what is asked of him scholastically, so he turns to mischief. Now that you understand how his brain works, you can imagine the havoc he can create. Against all odds, some dyslexics survive school and become very successful, but unfortunately, other dyslexic's wind up in jail. Dottie, Dougie's dyslexic sister, and other female dyslexics, often melt into the background. They may internalize their frustration and feel stupid or insecure. What a loss of potential! *The point is that the dyslexics in your classroom or home will either take your time and energy to help them excel or they will take your time and energy in management and damage control issues.* A stitch in time saves nine … an ounce of prevention … okay, no more of that! The Texas Dyslexia Law and others like it are proving that if dyslexia is understood, the students are remediated at an early age and they are given the accommodations they need to excel, that they actually wind up costing much less money and demanding less negative energy then students who are left to flounder.

The world today can be a hostile environment for a dyslexic, but it does not have to be. I know none of us want them to be. My goal in writing this section was to provide you with a few concrete ideas to help you change that, one dyslexic at a time. More importantly, it was to create understanding and a change in thinking, so that we can all be enriched by the precious dyslexic students we live near or serve.

Explore the Huge Dyslexia Hall of Fame

Please research amazing dyslexics. Find dyslexics that have excelled in areas your student or friend is interested in. Read their stories. Study their accomplishments. Talk about the strengths your dyslexic has in common with some of them. Discuss how these hall of famers achieved greatness despite some of their limitations and how they capitalized on the amazing parts of being dyslexic.

Moms Rock

A final note is an encouragement to mothers of dyslexic children. Statistically, dyslexics who excel in school and even more importantly, in life, almost always have a mother in the wings who is their champion. (Of course, Dads are important too!) Do not ever discount your role in your child's life … whether you are educated or not … dyslexic or not! Stand up and be the voice for your dyslexic children and help them reach for the stars!

We have added 4 men to our little family. (With another little man on the way) Our grandkids have a high chance of being dyslexic. This team of people you see in the picture above will have the challenge of being sure our grandkids understand dyslexia, know if they are dyslexic or not, and if they are, then we will need to find the tools they specifically need to learn as a dyslexic in our world. With the Lord's help, we are up to the challenge! We hope you are too for your loved ones.

The hot older man in the picture above is the best father and husband in the world. He is the only non-dyslexic in our original family group! Through our entire journey he has been our rock, our cheerleader, and our support. His faith in God and in us has given us so much strength as we faced each battle! We are grateful beyond words for him and dedicate this book to our wonderful worker man – Tim Mandon

Writing this book has been a 20-year process. Our youngest thought of the title in the middle of the night when she was five. She is twenty-five, married, and a first-grade teacher now. For 15 years we have been sharing this information with teachers, parents, friends and even strangers via email and printed copies, all the while adding to the content. The struggle we went through educating our dyslexic daughters was hard and long. We faced different challenges each year. We still face challenges living in a world designed for non-dyslexics. We were not bragging when we told you about our successes. We were hoping to provide inspiration for anyone dealing with dyslexia. We also enjoy sharing all the amazing benefits we enjoy because of the way our brains were designed. We live such fun, dynamic, creative, interesting, and successful lives because of and despite of our dyslexia! Our goal is that this book gives you hope, acceptance, and understanding – for others or yourself.

Resources

To write this book, I had many wells to draw from. The wisdom and knowledge I have gained through twenty years of lectures, conversations with educators, tutors and parents have enriched my life. Experiences with students, my family, and my own life have been priceless. Here are some of resources that helped us along the way.

Overcoming Dyslexia: A New and Complete Science-Based Program for Reading Problems at Any Level by Sally Shaywitz, M.D.
This was a fascinating book and I have realized that a lot of what I have learned about dyslexia is based on her research. It is pretty hard to read, so I got it on CD.

The Dyslexic Scholar: Helping Your Child Succeed in the School System by Kathleen Nosek
This is full of information on what your rights are as a parent and what the schools are required to provide for your student.

Thank You, Mr. Falker by Patricia Polacco
This is a wonderful story that tells the story of the author as a child with dyslexia! A great gift for a caring teacher!

Henry Winkler (the FONZ) is dyslexic and has published great books for dyslexic kids.

Rick Riordan wrote a fantastic series called The Lightning Thief. The hero in the story is dyslexic and my kids loved that.

I listen to tons of TED Talks and podcasts on dyslexia.

Bright Solutions for Dyslexia Website is an amazing resource. Reading it and listening to lectures by Susan Barton have been invaluable.

Dyslexics learn best using a program that is based on the Orton-Gillingham Approach to Teaching Reading. You can research this approach. It is fascinating. *A multisensory program is imperative for a dyslexic learner.* Barton Reading and Spelling, that was mentioned before, is based on these principles. Other curriculums that are worth looking into are:

- Logic of English
- All About Reading and All About Spelling
- Phonetic Zoo
- Touch-Type-Read-Spell
- Nessy Reading and Spelling
- Lexia

Reading with your child is so important! It is also important to find books that your struggling reader can read independently but aren't boring or too juvenile for their age. I want to share some book series for early readers (K-4) and older struggling readers.

For Young Readers

I love Magic Tree House, Who Is, and Cam Jansen! I have heard Mr. Putter and Tab is another cute series.

These are other suggestions:

- Acorn Books

- Penguin Young Readers

- Ready to Read (Great series is Henry and Mudge)

- Green Light Readers - Books have audio book link! (Great Series is Iris and Walter)

- Step into Reading

- Half Pint Readers -These are controlled texts that each focus on a specific set of sounds and go well with specific lessons you are doing for extra practice. (Repetition is very important for dyslexic learners) These are also good for students who are struggling readers and need reinforcement of specific sounds.

- Primary Phonics Story Book Sets - These are controlled texts that each focus on a specific set of sounds and go well with specific lessons for practice.

- My First Phonics Library - Usborne

- My First Reading Library - Usborne (Really cool because one page has harder words and is created for the parent to read and the next page has smaller words for the student, so you read the books together. Also good for students who are struggling readers and need reinforcement of specific sounds.)

Older Struggling Readers

- High Noon Books sells Sound Out Chapter Books
- Voyager Sopris sells SuperCharger Readers
- Simple Words sell Decodable Readers

Communication with teachers is crucial. Attitude is everything in life and is particularly important when addressing teachers. They are in a tough position with many different student's needs to take into consideration. Most teachers have not been educated on dyslexia, just as I had not been. I am so happy that this seems to be changing. Some states are even adding early screening for dyslexics into their educational framework. I believe most teachers have all their student's best interest at heart and ***deserve to be addressed with this in mind***. Appreciation and understanding go a long way when asking your teachers to learn about dyslexia and help you help your student to succeed in school. This is a letter I emailed to my daughter's teachers. This is the one I sent to High School teachers. You can personalize it for any grade and email it to your child's teachers. I CC'ed the school guidance counselor as well when I sent this letter. I always requested a response. If I did not get one, I would resend it or call.

Dear Teachers,

Hi! Thanks for all your hard work! We are very thankful for the job you do. We are writing our children's teachers to inform you that our three daughters are dyslexic. They have had tons of help, are very bright and are extremely hard workers, but you can imagine how hard school is these days for them. Unfortunately, most people don't really know what it means to be dyslexic, and most people would not guess that Sarah, Katie, and Bethany had any major learning issues - so the girls have taken some very embarrassing hard hits in class. It may appear that the girls are not trying, listening, or that they are being lazy. None of that is the case.

First, I am a teacher and a dyslexic. I did not understand dyslexia as a classroom teacher. No one taught me the facts in college. When my kids had a hard time learning to read – I began my research. Here is a nutshell of 13 years of learning.

Dyslexic brains work differently in three ways:

1. **Information Processing:** An average brain stores and retrieves information down well-established nerve paths- (I call it a speed train track) and there is a special area in the brain made for processing that information that is easy to access on the train. Dyslexic brains process information using the 4-wheel drive method. Information is stored in random places and therefore harder to retrieve. There is no trail to the language center, so a dyslexic is constantly having to decode each word.

   How this affects them negatively in school: It is extremely hard to call up random facts, (names, dates, words, formulas, tables, how to spell something, grammar/other rules, formats, ETC), Because of their creative thinking, they can thing of many ways to misbehave! Reading takes forever. Fluent reading out loud is hard. Reading uses a ton of energy for them.

How this affects them positively in school: They are usually amazing thinkers, very creative, outside the box problem solvers, see lots of angels, understand the big picture, are great leaders, and are intuitive!

Little ways to help: You can teach using songs, stories, rhymes, give them a 3x5 card where they can write out facts to use during a test, give them word banks for tests, link learning to hand motions or anything multisensory, give them more time on assignments or tests, don't count off for spelling on in class work.

2. **Auditory Processing**: An average brain can see a word and break it into individual sounds and then put it back together in a flash. A dyslexic brain sees/hears sounds fine but cannot pull them apart.

   How this affects them negatively in school: They have an extremely hard time decoding and reading new material out loud, spelling is almost impossible when you cannot break apart sounds, and they may have a hard time reading out loud.

   How this affects them positively in school: Hmmm … not so much!!!

   Little ways to help: Don't dock for spelling errors if they had no chance to get help with spelling (like on in class writing projects or tests), don't force them to read out loud, and give them more time for reading assignments.

3. **Directionality:** Dyslexics have no internal compass. Left/right/ up /down/forward/backward/ are all very confusing to a dyslexic. This is where the common misconception that dyslexics see things backwards come from. They see fine - they just process things directionally wrong.

How this affects them negatively in school: Spelling, (In what order do those vowels go?), order of operations, transposing letters, numbers, steps, dates, time periods, mixing up names, etc.

How this affects them negatively in school: Often very good at sports and VAPA (They do things a new way that no one is expecting and that is often very wonderful!)

Little ways to help: understand the spelling issue, give them ways to memorize steps in order that are multisensory, acknowledge when they get a concept right, but just transposed something in an answer, understand when they "get it", but don't remember a few details

I really appreciate the time you just took to understand my kids. Approximately 1 in 5 kids is dyslexic, so a big chunk of your students are having the same struggles as my kids. Lots of dyslexics never get any help and that is so sad and such a loss of potential. If you ever want more information o the subject- I'd love to give you a copy of a cool book we wrote on the subject.

Each of my kids has been driven to tears in a classroom by a teacher who I am sure had good intentions. If you ever have an issue with our daughters - please let us know. We would love to support both of you in this amazing learning journey of high school. We truly are so grateful for teachers and all they do.

Please email or call us to let us know you received this information.

Thanks!

Communicating that you are on the same team and are 100% interested in partnering with the teacher and school to make school the best learning experience for your student is what I have found to be the most effective. However, knowing your rights is important as well. I never let my kids be retained because statistically that is not a productive solution in the long run. In a few cases I did not let my children take state testing because of the stress testing was having on them at that specific time in their academic journey. I requested less homework in the lower grades when my children were doing extra tutoring for dyslexia. (Getting this tutoring at school is ideal, but it was not available to my daughters. We paid for it ourselves. I also quit my job and homeschooled the girls for specific times in each of their educational journeys. These were big sacrifices and I realize not everyone can make them. We were able to make them and it was worth it to us.) Getting your student assessed at school can be helpful. If dyslexics qualify for help through the school, they usually get a 504. That means that your child can get accommodations specific to their learning needs. One of my three daughters had one. I wish I had done evaluations on all my daughters at school and had gotten them 504's, but we decided not to at the time. If they have a 504 you can get them help easier since the help is mandated and not up to the individual teacher, and your student can also get extra time on SAT/ACTs. A 504 or IEP can also help you get accommodations automatically in college. Some helpful accommodations to request for a dyslexic student are multisensory phonics remediation, more time on assignments and tests, adjusting the length of assignments, adjusted grading on spelling and grammar, ability to type or use voice to text features instead of hand writing assignments, word lists or information note cards for testing, separate testing rooms, copies of someone's notes, books on audio, and anything else that helps compensate for the specific challenges their dyslexia pose in your students ability to learn and perform in school.

Thanks for letting us share our journey with you. We wish you the best as you explore the wonders and pitfalls of dyslexia yourself or with someone you love. We would love to hear from you. Contact the authors at randohouse5@gmail.com